Available Soon

Conversations of the Soul in Polish & Spanish

Rozmowy Duchowe

Convercaciones Del Almas

The Pain Monster's Gift — a memoir

CONVERSATIONS OF THE SOUL

A Poet's Journey from Pain to Peace

ELIZABETH HELEN ROSE

"Oh Eternal Spring, in a waterless place I found you."

For booking - www.elizabethhelenrose.com.

© *Conversations of the Soul*

Copyright © 2020 by Elizabeth Helen Rose

This title available wherever books are sold.

1st edition ISBN 978-1-7360-468-0-7

All scripture quotations, unless otherwise indicated, are taken from the Holy Bible, New International Version ^{R}, NIV ^{R}. Copyright © 1973, 1978, 1984 by Biblica, Inc. ^{TM} Used by permission. All rights reserved worldwide.

No part of this book may be reproduced in any form or by any electronic or mechanical means, including information storage & retrieval systems, without written permission from the author, except for use of brief quotations in book review.

Cover design —Elizabeth Helen Rose & Jessica Faenza; Photo-Art — created in Microsoft PictureIt®™, Photo Lab®™ and Adobe Photoshop®™ by the author. Photos: Pain —Allen Schaarschmidt; Almost & Sisters — Grace Hermann; Author's portraits & Preserves —Jessica Faenza

Printed in the United States of America

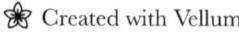 Created with Vellum

*To my soulmate-husband,
two people wrapped in one special being,
part human, part angel.*

*"Pastor Al" of
Blessed Hope Church of the Nazarene
Phillipsburg, New Jersey
Warren County Chaplain - Amedisys Hospice
USMC two-purple heart, almost-amputee
combat veteran, dog handler
3rd Marine Division, 1st Battalion*

*Thank you for your tender care
when my arms hung, like dead wood, at each side.
You walked, side by side, step by step, with me.
You personified unconditional love as you dressed,
fed and drove me, near and far, to seek help.*

*Without you, I would have imploded.
I love you.*

❤

Acknowledgments

My sincerest gratitude to my:

~Creator who spun the miracle and brought back, from the dead, my arms, at eighty percent capacity. Without His mercy this book would have died at conception.

~Support teams, to you who have lifted, even one finger, for a prayer, for a chore, to lighten our load.

~Family -- nuclear, extended and church.

>For your infinite love, constant prayers and endless patience.

>Al — for your courage in our-life's trenches.

>Jay, daughter #1, graphic designer, proofreader extraordinaire and owner of Blu-Jay Transportation—for your pedal-to-the-metal graphic-art deliverance, and MANY other, rescues.

>Heather, daughter #2, mud-runner, medical research writer and owner of Rite-Idea — for pain creams, CBD oils, your cheesecake medicine, anytime I asked for it —and so much more.

>Grandkids, for carving a permanent heart, in my heart, that no hand of wind or time can erase.

>Siblings, siblings in-law, nieces, nephews and cousins —for your love and prayers, your wisdom and sense of humor. And to some of you, for your generous support of our ministry. Thank you for the family reunions, the Gap Diner breakfasts, the wonderful trips, holiday meals, get togethers, cards, calls and texts. And the FaceTimes!

>Church family – for your forty-year dedication to our *third child*, Blessed Hope. We couldn't take care of her without you. To the NYI youth group — You made me laugh, drove me crazy, ate me out of church-house and home. You medicine'd the pain out of me on days when I couldn't make it.

~Dr. James M. Hunter, who died in 2013. Orthopedic surgeon at Thomas Jefferson University Hospital in Philadelphia for fifty years, pioneer in the field of hand surgery, who treated me and many patients with ultra kindness; trained more than 100 fellows in hand surgery. Editor of *Rehabilitation of the Hand and Upper Extremity*[1], the bible textbook of hand surgery and therapy.

~Dr. Stephan H. Whitenack, my thoracic surgeon in 1999 at Chestnut Hill Hospital in Philadelphia who allowed me to pray with him and his two nurses, prior to my operation, which had a bleak 13% recovery rate. I received his gift of compassionate answers to my million nervous questions at each visit. I am forever grateful for his successful surgery.

~All the super kind physical therapists —my tear wipers, who opened their hearts and gave me a soft place to land my careening heart. Core Physical Therapy, Chestnut Hill Rehab and Good Shepherd Rehab.

~Muzzy, Heather's Aussie Shepherd, who died in 1998, prior to my medical procedure. He adopted me as his best friend when my dead arms flopped around, and I could do nothing except walk, cry, pray and sing. He did it all, happily, with me.

~Laurel Wenson, author and teacher, who embraced me as her publishing mentee. What encouragement and help on my road to the land of ebooks, print publications, barcodes and beyond! www.laurelwenson.com.

~Anna Kierzkiewicz , poet and mother of five, on her expertise as she edited my Polish translation.

∼

Poetry peels away layers of intellect,
strips the pretense and reveals the naked soul.

Elizabeth Helen Rose

Contents

Foreword	xv
Introduction	xvii
1. Pain	1
2. Surrender	4
3. Confusion	5
4. Anguish	6
5. Obedience	10
6. Anger	12
7. Grace	14
8. Childhood	18
9. Dreams	22
10. Waiting	23
11. Words	25
12. Slander	27
13. Journey	29
14. Soul	32
15. Mama	34
16. Prayer	38
17. Kindness	40
18. Youth	44
19. Strength	48
20. Nature	50
21. Love	52
22. Time	56
23. Friend	57
24. Suffering	60
25. Music	62
26. Silence	63
27. Hope	64
28. Gift	68
29. Almost	76
30. Sin	80
31. Baggage	82

32. Parents	86
33. Freedom	90
34. Savior	94
35. Fear	96
36. Wisdom	98
37. Archer	100
38. Sisters	104
39. Artist	108
40. Soulmate	110
41. Obstacle	111
42. Papa	114
43. Graduate	118
44. Husband	122
45. Regret	126
46. Procrastination	128
47. Familiarity	131
48. Daughter	134
49. Joy	138
50. Courage	142
51. Accolade	146
52. Death	148
53. Forgiveness	150
54. Skin	151
55. Marriage	153
56. Distributors	154
57. Faith	156
58. Contentment	158
59. Fulfillment	161
60. Peace	164
61. Preserves	166
Notes	171
Index - Alphabetical	173
Epilogue	175
About the Author	179

CONVERSATIONS OF THE SOUL

Foreword

I'm Elizabeth's husband for the past fifty-two wonderful years, a Pastor and a former U.S. Marine who returned home from Vietnam severely wounded. I mention this because I've never seen anyone, myself included, handle their pain the way Elizabeth has and continues to do so.

Her poetry chronicles her journey through her pain, emotionally, spiritually and physically. My hope is that her poems will uplift you and that you will know that your pain does not define you, nor does it have to defeat you.

I've been an eyewitness to her journey, and my admiration of what she has conquered has no bounds. I hope as you read her writings that you, too, will receive encouragement as I have, and still do, from her perseverance as she continues to fight this battle everyday, victoriously. —Rev. Allen Schaarschmidt

Semper Fi, my love.

Introduction

In 1995, at age forty-seven, I slowly descended into the hell of ungodly pain and idleness. The torture began with an annoying muscle burn in my right bicep, which spread and grew worse. I went from doctor to doctor, from medical test to medical test with no answers. The severe burn in my arms and neck, the constant jabs and insomnia became my daily companions.

After being examined by eight physicians over a one-and-a-half year period, with no results, my husband drove me to the Hunter Hand and Nerve Clinic in Philadelphia. There, after a third, but more comprehensive, EMG, seventy-four-year-old Dr. Hunter diagnosed me with Thoracic Outlet Syndrome, also known as Brachial Plexopathy.

TOS affects the nerves and blood vessels in the neck. It can be brought on in various ways such as trauma, as in the case of football or in vehicular accidents. It can happen at birth when a baby's arm is stretched too far. Or it can occur through repetitive use, like typing for extended periods, as in my case.

By the time I saw Dr. Hunter, the nerve damage was permanent. My dominant right arm hung at my side, like dead wood with constant zaps of electric shocks. My left arm followed close behind. We lived in medical waiting rooms.

One by one, my beloved activities, like playing the piano and conducting the church choir vanished. Headaches blinded me and often drove me to nausea. Our once-clean home turned into a cluttered mess. Clean piles of laundry waited to be folded on the dining room table. Dust balls rolled across the hardwood floor. Dirty dishes sat on the counter and sink.

The inability to wipe my runny nose or wipe my constant tears or hold a book to read made me crazy. Not only the pain, but the idleness had beat me down. I wanted to die.

Introduction

One morning, in May of 1997, when I reached the end of my capacity to handle the pain, I dropped to my knees at a kitchen chair, laid my head on the seat and howled, like a wild animal. When I finished howling, I prayed.

> *God, if this is how you want me, then fine; I'll accept it, but don't let me just sit here in self-pity. Don't let me waste a minute of this. Let me learn whatever it is you want me to learn and move on. Give me a job. Give me purpose.*

I struggled to my feet; my arms dangled. My hair had plastered itself to my face with the mucus from my nose and tears from my eyes. I couldn't wipe my face. I bent over a sour, rumpled towel on the kitchen counter and rotated my face back and forth to wipe it. Then I shuffled into the living room and slumped onto sofa. I laid down on my belly and dropped my left arm toward my Bible that lay on the floor. With one haphazard swing I swiped it open. Psalm 77:14 stared up at me.

"You are the God who performs miracles."

I squinted and read it again. Hope, like condensation, seeped into my heart. I reached for a scrap of paper and a pencil. With my better left hand, I scratched out an almost legible note: *5/20/97 My Miracle*. I thought about my sorry condition for a moment and added the words *in faith*. I tucked the note between the pages at Psalm 77.

When Spring came, and I was capable of doing nothing, I decided to walk everyday. I slept in jogging clothes and walked the fields that way, ungroomed, till my husband, Al, came home to shower me. Soon I added prayer to my walks and then singing. Psalm 77 became the foundation of my daily spiritual regimen. Each day I made a conscious effort to focus on all the good things God had given me in the past.

During these prayer walks my mind would flood with thoughts and my heart would fill with hope. In order to save the phrases that popped into my head I memorized them as I walked. The words

Introduction

tasted like sweet morsels to me. I'd gather them in the basket of my mind, and then race home to pour the contents into an old tape recorder. Captured in small increments these thoughts grew into this manuscript, *Conversations of the Soul*.

Here's what amazed me then and amazes me still, two decades later. Though debilitated and in severe pain, I felt strangely liberated. I had a purpose. My new mission became to not waste this painful experience. God walked me through the Valley of Sorrow and introduced me to His strength, peace and joy. I wanted to document that journey.

In 1999 I underwent surgery (with a meager 13% success rate) with Dr. Stephan Whitenack at Chestnut Hill Hospital in Philadelphia, Pennsylvania. I thank God for his successful operation and for the return of a good measure of relief. I'm grateful for the joy of dressing myself again and for the ability to brush my teeth. What joy to eat like an adult instead of a messy toddler! Although my arms still face challenges, and I'm unable to return to the former physical me, my life has a new perspective. Not only are two scalene muscles in my neck gone, something else is gone - taking life for granted.

I get to share life's simple truths and verses from my poems wherever I go. The response has overwhelmed me. Getting the words on paper has been a slow journey. Along the way I stumbled into numerous rest stops; some I didn't choose. I thank God for technology and the patient tech-support kids who guided me, over the phone, when my speech-recognition software and foot-pedal mouse failed. I thank God for my husband-hero, who rushed to my rescue each time technology went haywire. Without him these poems would have collected dust on old cassettes in a drawer.

I hope the words in this book inspire you to accomplish something positive with your pain. Invite God into your Valley of Sorrow and prepare for a miracle.

—Elizabeth Helen Rose (Niemoczynski) Schaarschmidt, Easton, Pennsylvania

Pain

Even in the night,
when the arms of sleep
have finally rocked me still,
you rouse me.
Why?

In the dark I wince
at your loathsome presence.
Your fingers jab me.
Monster!
My daily companion.

Are we a pair?
A duo? --linked forever
by one misfortune?
Here we lie,
shackled together.

You exasperate me!
You drive me mad
because where
I go, you go also.
You clink your chain and
I must follow.

But
you have limits.
And I
have boundaries.

ELIZABETH HELEN ROSE

However hard you try;
however far you stretch
your tentacles;
you may grope for, but
never reach

that private room,
that sacred place,
where I can go,
where One stands guard,
The Master
of my soul.

∼

-April, 1997

Surrender

Oh Lord.
My battle weary heart
raises the white flag
of surrender.

It falls to its knees,
head bowed,
and waits to be carried
with the wounded.

Far too long
it has resisted;
too hard it has fought
to wrench itself free,
not from an enemy,

who attacks from without,
but from Your Will,
from your outstretched arms,
whose embrace does not confine;
rather, sets free
all that you are in me.

Confusion

Stop!
You can't come in.
I've slammed the door,
bolt fastened.

Stay!
Outside, on the
exterior remain with
the rest of the noisy traffic,
those blaring horns of
doubt and fear.

Here, in privacy,
I choose to bathe.
Chin raised, eyes closed,
I slip my soul
into the warm bath
of Divine silence.

Into God's
liquid love I submerge
my soul, and on
His gentle ebb and flow, I drift
toward His promise
of deliverance,
the buoy that upholds
me.

Anguish

Like a lost lamb,
I bellow for my flock,
but the earthbound have no ears
for this kind of bleating.

My shrieks have scraped
my vocal chords of all song,
my voice, just a rasp
across granite now.

Open your ears,
you hearing-impaired!
I sleep on stones!
Fingers of pain
jab me day and night!

Pick me up! Take me home!
Save me from this ghastliness!
Must I stumble through
another night of sleepless hell?

Must I wander,
mouth agape, eyes bulged,
arms paralyzed, dangling --my
tangled hair mucus'd on my face?

I've scaled every
medical mountain.
My search for a cure brings me
here, to this morning's
deserted rock canyon.

CONVERSATIONS OF THE SOUL

Once, my faith,
like a slingshot built from
Lignum Vitae[1]
shot my pleas to heaven,
way beyond your canyon walls.

But today,
my prayers nose-dive,
plunge straight down,
into your ravine.

And Heaven?
The place where my voice
once reached The Shepherd?
--seems utterly remote.

Enough
to pain, I say.
Go ahead, dig
your heel into my nape,
press my face into
this rock.

I will
prostrate if I must,
but my heart rests on
The Savior's
bed of promise.
I wait
for victory,
for glory.

Obedience

Lord, it's *You*!
How the minute vibrations
of your whisper
rupture the stonewall
of my
self-centeredness!

My heart sat,
chin up, arms crossed,
with a pout,
inside my self-erected
blockade.

Until
You whispered.
Then it turned around.
Not to amplify
the sound,
nor to identify
the voice,

but to hearken,
to yield,
to run,
to kneel
at your feet.

Awesome Power!
Eminent Expression!
Holy Profundity!
Sacred Mystery!
Master!

Anger

Not even
the slightest upward turn
at the corners of your mouth,
no smile to grace
your lovely face.

Into your eyes,
a frozen tundra, I gaze.
Your brow, the furrowed ridge,
that pain's avalanche
has left behind.

Setbacks,
layers upon layers
of sorrow,
too heavy, too slippery
to hold
each other up
upon life's slope,
have given way.

Bereft of hope,
your heart has somersaulted
within a hurtling mass
of tumult and
despair.

Then,
your cold silence.
Your joy,
buried under ice.
Gladness frozen deep
beneath.

CONVERSATIONS OF THE SOUL

Till.
The Comforter comes.
The Emmanuel.
The *God with Us.*
His warmth is
warm enough to melt away
a *lifetime's* worth
of ice and snow.

He thaws your deep-freeze.
Your winter softens
into Spring.
He resurrects what died.
Your barren slopes
re-bloom
into color again.

And, the
long-awaited
butterflies
of joy and gladness
flutter back
to alight upon your
soul.

Grace

From
my apex, at age 47,
at the peak of my rush hour,
to the ground, my
face into dirt,
life spit me
out.

I, the
broken-winged
sparrow, blinked up at my
intact buddies who
winged toward
blue sky.

Daily downpours
of sorrow pelted me.
When floods reached beak level,
your plane-ticket-gift
arrived.

From aircraft into
your airport's human river
--heads bobbing, luggage rolling—
my jitters stepped in,
empty handed

though my heart,
(under my vest,
with its pockets stuffed)
clutched a plane load
of anxiety.

CONVERSATIONS OF THE SOUL

As I scanned
the crowded gate
for absent you, the current
tried to take me
downstream.

I bit my lip.
My gaze fell.
Maybe you forgot.
Then, bam! --your red roses
exploded into my
downcast face.

You scooped me
from the surge and grinned
sister medicine into me.
Your double row of pearly whites,
Heaven's first-aid kit.

Up the stairs,
into your guestroom,
you ushered and un'suitcased me.
From pain's mud, you lifted me
to your bird sanctuary,

to where
floods evaporate,
to where broken wings heal,
to where *the damaged* can hear
pans rattle and bacon fry;

to where a bird
can sense God's feet
scurry inside a sister's slippers,
and feel sure that the
footsteps one hears belong
to the Savior.

You nursed me,
sleeves rolled up, apron on.
And when the time
came for me to go,
you placed me up
upon the wings of prayer
where I could fly.

-For Grace - 2000

Childhood

Design
me a home
where walls don't divide,
but multiply my vast
possibilities.

Give me
strong-muscled
load bearers,
that hold planets
within reach.

Give me
book-holders with
arms like super-magnets
that pull a kid into
worlds exotic and unique.

Give me
rock walls for the
clench, for the climb, to
bone up on strength
and confront my fear.

Give me
easel walls,
vessels into which pain
can be dumped
and art can be born.

CONVERSATIONS OF THE SOUL

For the
rover in me give
road, street and trail maps,
themed, astronomy
and world maps.

Give me
Some blank walls
for graffiti,
for the throw of paint,
for the play of light,
of shadow.

Build for me
window walls,
peek-throughs and movables,
for when I want to see
or be seen.

Purpose walls, like
aquarium or garden or waterfall,
to trigger the
love of fish
or flower.

Give me space,
in between and among,
where freedom
doesn't let go, but
holds tight my liberty.

Take me
to places where
discovery won't maim,
but will create
the wonderful
I was born to be.

Open
your ear to *my* song.
It's not off key, but
in harmony
with my
individuality.

Feed me
with food that doesn't
just fill, but fulfill, the
a m a z i n g
in me to be.

Dreams

There...
within the deepest recesses
of my soul, my children,
waiting in the wings
of heaven
for the journey
to be born.

What stopped you
from coming through,
to grow in my
daylight's possibility?

Did you shipwreck
in utero? – in my
stormy sea of hopelessness?

Open
your tiny eyes
while
I unwrap you, now.
There...
my dreams
to be.

Waiting

You're
the quiet one,
my middle child, the
in-between
of my birth and death.

To a
temporary post
my Maker has summoned you
to usher me
from back there
to somewhere.

Sandwiched
between
my start and my finish,
you bring me
numbered days, opportunities
to make a positive
difference.

During your stay,
in between
my dawn and my dusk,
we'll engage, at times, with the
insurmountable.

Melt me, mold me.
But place me
in Holy Fire.
Upon my Maker's anvil
lay me down.
Let *His* hand
direct each blow.

Teach
me to rejoice,
to celebrate this middle,
however long or
short or
grim.

For one mid-day,
mid-night, mid-heartbeat,
my Maker will blow
the fire out.

I want
His hand to lift me,
His lips to blow
earth's dust
from me.

I want
His smile on you,
my waiting,
on you, my costly in-between,
His handiwork
polished,
His design rendered,
His image
reflected in me.

Words

Like
citrus bites,
orange or grapefruit, you
juice-drench
the parched buds
of my tongue.

You!
— tangy morsels that
zap my soul,
slap my senses,
numbed by pain,
wide awake.

From
The Ancient Tree,
dendron, with fruit, heavy laden,
by Living-Water hydrated,
I pluck you from
The Pages
in daybreak's hush,
one by one.

Deep
within the pockets
of my heart
I tuck you and wait
for you to
ripen.

When
I take you out?
When
I cut you
apart?
The fragrance!

When
I pair you with
non-citrus?
—an apple, a pear!
what zest you add.

Out of
your many,
from Heaven's outgrowth,
I select a few,
create a combo and
savor
each exotic flavor.

No matter
a drought or a flood,
nor today's bitter winter,
when I open the Book of Plenty,
I reap a bounty.

Slander

Your tongue
fondles gossip like
my tongue nuzzles ice cream
in July heat.

For truth
you have no appetite.
You hear one thing worthy,
and you cringe.

Devil!
Angel mask
over features twisted.
You bid my dearest friend
for a hearsay
lunch.

Fiend!
The word spells
friend minus the r.
You knife my back, cut
me to the depth
of my soul.

Murderer!
Our friendship dies.
You intended me for slaughter,
but a Golden Cord
reels in my soul.

On a
white steed He
thunders in.
My Comforter.
He bullwhips the blade
of your tongue
from between your
teeth.

Healer!
He bears Heavenly resin.
I stagger till
His balm
fills up my core,
where the
arms of mortal solace
cannot reach.
And then I stand.

Journey

How unharnessed,
all of us, young, back then.
We convertible'd with
our hair flying,
till a bend in the road
diverted me.

My buddies
made headway;
their engines roared past me
who catapulted into
a stonewall.

I watched them
fade; how I longed to go
in their direction.
My heart still beats the drum
of our togetherness.

Now rehab
couples me to strangers whose
movements falter,
just like mine.
Upon a fixed course,
like a railcar,
the rehabbers and I
roll on rails
fastened to the ground.

But I consider this:
Somewhere to some kind
of path —by chance,
by choice,
to rails,
perhaps unseen,
or even predetermined,
we all get constrained.

Therefore:
I choose to fix
my gaze not down
upon the rails,
but upward, outward,
toward *His Horizon*.

There
my destination lies.
And you?
The Journey?
Well,
God's Auto Pilot
has me,
and I smile as
God and I
enjoy the ride.

Soul

My *body* is the mist.
You, my soul, are the *fire*.
You ignite yet
don't burn us down.

You live,
with or without a body.
The nano-second
you exit?
My body evaporates.

You come without lips,
without vocals of your own,
yet we converse
in our private language
of stillness.

When we get alone,
body and soul undress;
our hands peel off and drop
the day's troubles.

I hand you
my inaudible moans,
my mute laughter,
my silent giggles, my
invisible tears,
my bottled anger, my
hushed awe,
my unspoken fear.
And you take it all.

CONVERSATIONS OF THE SOUL

You,
my dear fire,
my mystery,
invisible to mortals,
but visible to The Eternal, you burn
to create, not consume.

Enigma!
We are separate, yet
we walk as one.
Seventy winters ago, you
ignited my tiny zygote.
He who powers the universe
sent you with the
flame of my
existence.

∼

Mama

How
tranquil now,
how untroubled, here
in front of me,
your busy hands
lie still.

My mind looks
past you in your coffin,
toward your garden,
at us, the
tender seedlings
in your care.

Just now,
I realize what a gift,
how rich
an endowment,
you have been to me.

When others
gave up, fled in the
midst of
tribulation,
you stayed, on
knees bent,
and pruned us all.

CONVERSATIONS OF THE SOUL

Only
this minute do I
know, without doubt,
that you live.
I feel you more
than ever.

My soul
genuflects.
My heart lifts
you high, as I strive to
cultivate a garden
of my own.

The seeds
I sow I take from
plants
your tireless hands
have sown
throughout the years
within my soul.

For Maria Regina
Rogulska Niemoczynski
1916-1992
Ambassador of the Poor
Nazi Labor Camp Survivor
Lover of Freedom
Prayer Warrior

Prayer

Toward
your cloister I inch.
With Faith and Doubt.
Into your seclusion I tiptoe.
My heart drags
two black garbage bags
of woe,
its arms
maxed out.

With
difficulty, a load far
too heavy for
a heart to hold,
I stumble
at your door.

Doubt halts.
Faith slips.
I stutter; my words crumble.
Doubt grabs a hammer,
pounds a nail, starts to
build a barricade
to you.

I whisper a plea.
My faith creeps forward.
I murmur.
Faith sneaks past the barrier,
breaks into a run,
cries aloud!
My agony bleeds
for mercy.

CONVERSATIONS OF THE SOUL

So unapparent is His
approach that I never see nor feel
The Hands
that take the bags
from me.

His presence,
like incense, wafts and lingers
long after we've cooled your embers,
long after My Maker has
set me free.

Kindness

Like a shovel,
you jab the sun-baked clay
of bitterness
packed down by
time.

Your blade
cuts and turns
rancor gathered,
each offense clinging to
the other,
till a heart loses its
ability to beat.

I pronounce you
Spade with Noble Purpose,
Tiller of Parched Ground,
tooled by
The Master himself.

Your edge
amputates hate.
One splinter
from your shaft is
worth more
than this world's
weight in gold.

Your reward can
only come
from Heaven!
What hand holds that vast
a prize?

CONVERSATIONS OF THE SOUL

Divine Shovel.
Earthly recognition pales
to that
which lies in store
for you inside
The Master's Shed.

Youth

Good-bye
sweet friend.
I've come to let
you go.

The ocean waves of
my memory rise and swell.
It's tide spills forth
our mementos.
Souvenirs of our juvenile
adventures
swirl ashore.

Remember when
your crayons flushed
my cheeks a thousand shades of pink?
When you stained my hair,
now washed in white,
a golden brown?

Outside the lines,
with shrieks and belly laughs,
how we colored
the humdrum,
the ivory pages
of our world!

CONVERSATIONS OF THE SOUL

I go to
befriend the pubescent
stranger, with shoulders wider,
with head higher,
whose feet step farther,
whose jitters I must
calm right now.

Farewell
dear friend.
The Hand who sets
the sun has
stretched your shadow
and cast your
fleeting image
in the sand.

Strength

Oh
Eternal Spring,
from your liquid treasure
my soul drinks
long.

Wash
the dryness,
cleanse the dust
from my sun-baked
heart.

In this
waterless place
I found you!
From pain's desert
you burst forth as I trekked
through this dry
Valley of Sorrow.

It's *here*
that you quenched
the thirst of
those
who passed before
me.

And it's
here you'll
wash away
the drought of those
who walk
behind.

Nature

Undaunted by
my selfishness, indifferent
to my neglect, you,
dear nature trail, greet me
at dawn with your smile on.

To your
open arms I run.
Your trillion pink and purple
waist-high petals, on each side of
this dirt path, embrace me.

From your
Spring renascence, a
Creator-patented well, my
senses drink, till my
ravenous soul distends.

How your rustling
soothes my restless heart! —
--when your breeze
fingers
the leaves—

--when your birds
chirp the lullabies that rock
my troubled soul
to sleep.

Love

A pure
and gentle mist,
like dew,
you gathered,
in microscopic droplets,
upon a bud not yet
in bloom.

Mysterious,
inexplicable as life itself,
your drops multiplied,
expanded over
time,
and created
one percolating stream
of energy.

When
did you burst
into today's deluge?
How did you grow into today's
swollen river?
Which drop
permeated
my heart until
it opened?

CONVERSATIONS OF THE SOUL

All these years
your formidable current
carried me,
engulfed my heart,
yet you never
drowned
me, the
fragile blossom
borne by you.

For Al on our 40th, 2008

Time

Why
do you rush me so?
What *is*
your hurry?

Can't you see?
Can you not discern
this ephemeral
dilemma of mine?

Just
a while longer,
let me stay
and tarry here.

You know
I won't recur,
not quite like this.
My brief episode will not
repeat itself.

I've asked
The Keeper of my clock
to slow them down,
my mortal strokes,
the beating
of my metronome.

There's much
to do, and I've been given
so precious little
of you.

Friend

What a contrast
between the festooned imitations,
the surrogates, and
you.

Ever smell
plastic flowers?
Elaborate.
Shapely.
Dazzling even.

Artificial colors
and textures; from manmade
composites the fakes
are synthesized.
Not you.

From a distance,
across a room, the lack of
resemblance, the
disparity between
you and a replica, may go
unnoticed.
So it goes with
people.

Only
when lives touch,
when paths converge does whatever
dwells inside of friends
emerge.

ELIZABETH HELEN ROSE

So it went with you.
Your truth lay
under your bark, at your
core, when life chainsawed you,
at age 35,
and you tumbled
to the ground.

Years later,
like a petal from a rose,
fallen and saved,
your memory drifts in,
and still emits your fragrance
that comforts me.

For Bob, 1993

Suffering

To your classroom,
to your autocratic manner
I came ill-equipped,
most
unprepared.

One fine day
your staccato steps
marched in and dislodged the
peace that sprawled
within my soul.

Dear Teacher,
I don't recall; I have no
inkling of
who enrolled me as
your student?
And why?

Yet front
and center, at this
school desk
I find myself seated;
your discourse bends my elbow,
to the task at hand.

Many
a teacher
made their mark,
embedded their facts,
carved their notch,
some deeper than others,
into my soul.

CONVERSATIONS OF THE SOUL

But, your hand,
has been the heaviest,
your truth, etched in me,
the deepest.

That your acrid
lessons I would come to
cherish most, is
the biggest
jolt of all.

Music

Like iced
lemonade that
splashes my
parched summer tongue;
you refresh me
that much!

You pour
your rhythm and blues
into my soul
and turn my slab
of stress
into melted butter.

I'll take
you either way,
cordial quiet or
with bubbles erupting.
Your intervals lift and relocate
my soul to new
surroundings.

No sooner
does your ice across
my upturned teeth clatter,
to announce your final
liquid measure?
I raise my glass.
Encore!

Silence

You are

Power
Weakness

Wisdom
Ignorance

Hero
Coward

Tribute
Defiance

Courage
Fear

Mute
Deafening

Hope

Despite
my lack of hospitality,
the mutters from
my mirthless soul,
you breeze in
as though invited.

All right then,
close the door.
You make me squint.
Please, kill the light that my walls
work hard to keep
out.

You want
to install what?
Glass?
As in a window?

Your offer,
like flint on steel,
strikes me; it ignites
this sequence of
events.

I nod,
grant permission.
Go ahead.
Just one pinhole,
though.

CONVERSATIONS OF THE SOUL

Your Finger,
lasers the partition,
skewers the barrier that
sequesters
me from sight.

More?
More.

More?
More.

More?
More.

More?
More!

∼

Gift

Yeah right.
Packaged as a
temporary visitor, he barged
in through my front door,
my daughter's
post-college roommate.

What was
I *s u p p o s e d* to do
when he moved in and had
nowhere to go?
He sashayed in
like he owned my place,
so I tolerated,
even cleaned up
after him.

He drove me nuts!
Me with my
zero tolerance for germs.
He and his love affair with dirt.
I craved order.
He relished chaos.

Our empty
nest became *his* all-night
slumber party,
my commuter traffic jam.

CONVERSATIONS OF THE SOUL

To have
mid-life crisis *a n d* this
now-entrenched
Don't-Sweat-the-Small-Stuff vagrant?
I don't think so!

Every time
he spotted me reaching for
my sneakers,
he'd beat me
to the front door, and
wait for me.

Did *I*
have the heart
to tell him, *thanks, but
I'd rather walk the nature trails
alone?*

You'd think
he would've appreciated
my good will
and at least wiped
his dirty feet
when we got back.

He made shy
puppy eyes at me.
In the beginning.
He'd mind his manners
too.

ELIZABETH HELEN ROSE

At first he just
ogled the snacks I munched
in front of him.
Then, of *c o u r s e* I shared.
I had no choice.
He was right there.
I just couldn't do it, eat
in front of somebody
like that.

It wasn't long
before he snooped around
the kitchen.
Took stuff that
didn't belong to him.

Hah!
I caught him sneakin'
food, right off the counter.
Stuffin' it in his mouth
behind my back!
He didn't see me
squint at him from the
corner.

One day,
out of the clear blue,
he *m a n h a n d l e d* me!
Gave me a bear hug.
'Bout took my breath away.
Forced me to laugh.
Out loud.

CONVERSATIONS OF THE SOUL

I had no idea he'd
been eavesdropping.
That year I cried a river.
He must've heard
the downpours.

His *Let's-Boogie*
philosophy
made him chase adventure
like a fourth-grade boy
headed for recess
after acing a math test
on a Friday afternoon.

How about
his crisis intervention?
Nothing is so bad
that a peanut butter sandwich
and a Frisbee
can't fix.
Get my drift?
(Did I mention
he drove me nuts?)

...so
I should have been
ecstatic when
they moved out on their own.
Everybody grows up.
(sigh)
I know that.

ELIZABETH HELEN ROSE

Privacy, order,
cleanliness returned.
The quiet reverberated
in our
hollow rooms.

But the worst
was yet to come.
The bad news bit
my heart like canines…
hit by a car?

The *a u d a c i t y*
of the unexpected.
Somewhere between
he barged in and *he died,*
my priorities had shifted.
Conceived in bedlam,
our relationship had flourished
despite my
countless protests.

How he changed
the constellation of my universe
and created
a revised edition of my heart.
Now *that's* the mystery.

The irony?
That his visit was a
heart-wrenching short one.
That his unspoken acts
of friendship taught me more
than words of
learned men.

CONVERSATIONS OF THE SOUL

That I fell
head-over-heels
in love
with this guy.
This gift from God,
this package

wrapped
in shedding fur,
this four-legged
tri-colored angel of mercy
and mischief and mayhem,
this whirling dervish
of devotion.

And I never knew
how much I loved him
till he died.

∼

For Muzzy – 1998

Almost

At your
portal I stand and
wait; my open arms, the cradle,
to receive her.
Just a few more
months.

But you
shoo me away, today,
empty-handed.
It's done,
you say.
Nuisance gone.

Your lips
blowtorch the news
into my chest.
I clench it!
And go up in flames.

My every
cell wails for the wonder
she would have been, for the
sacred process slashed,
for our angel
beheaded.

You
pilfered our joy!
You stole our Promise,
stripped the world of this treasure.
A jewel, gone!

CONVERSATIONS OF THE SOUL

Our
picture frames
embrace undeveloped film.
No sweet images,
of curls around her baby face;
just brown coated
gelatin strips of nothing,
take her place.

Have
you gone blind?
Can you not see my heart's
expenditure?
Can you not grasp the
detailed preparation,
for this
special birth
my heart has made?

*Let's go back to
the way we were,* you say?
How can I go back?
How do I return home?
The address has vanished!

The road on which
I came to you
has disappeared!
Fingers
not yet born;
hands too small to fight
abortion's blade
have struck
my soul!

ELIZABETH HELEN ROSE

Unwanted
by hassle, discarded
by inconvenience, Promise
lies cradled in a
landfill,
instead of a land filled
with love.

At Heaven's
portal, her Creator
takes her back, gift unopened,
blessing rejected,
life unfulfilled.

For Promise 2013

Sin

With one hiss,
you caress the plumes
of two egos.
Male and female.
Both are
married, but to
someone else.

To your
slick maneuvers,
to your
ulterior motives,
their ears clog;
their vows
vanish.

Just your
exaggeration,
your inflation of
their scant virtues hold
them captive.

Their pride
giggles over fake promises.
How playful
your
forked tongue.

On each other's
fine wrappings, their
Madison Avenue
packaging,
their eyes nibble.

CONVERSATIONS OF THE SOUL

Time passes.
Cravings expire.
That moment always comes.
Taste buds change.

By the time
their stomachs have
their fill,
each disguise nibbled away,
the truth lies
naked, noxious, foul.

Feathers lie
scattered everywhere;
their remnants bear witness,
to the songbird
family
that once lived
here.

For Peony , 1997

Baggage

Brand new,
molded and stamped,
we shot out
of life's
narrow opening
together.

Circumstance
and Choice.
Circumstance,
the burden.
Choice,
the gift.

From birth
I held you both, one
in each hand.
We trudged the distance,
endured miles of
wrinkled plans and
leaky promises.

Then, trouble
snapped your handles,
broke your latches.
So, I jerry-rigged
and hauled
your slippery cargo
till my soul
could haul no more.

CONVERSATIONS OF THE SOUL

That's when
I called
upon The Giver of
both the burden and
the gift.

The
Master Traveler
came. He repackaged my life,
bubblewrapped my breakables,
fixed the broken parts,
handed me kakis and
hiking boots.

What unknown
wilderness we've trod!
What rugged mountains
we've ascended!
Through many
a narrow passage
we have squeezed!

Circumstance and Choice.
A burden and a gift.
The Giver waits
to carry my burden,
if only I
choose to ask.

Parents

On this,
my commencement day,
I ascend the stage;
take my place
on the summit,
on the lime-lit pinnacle that
the public sees.

But I know,
I'm just a fraction,
a fragment
of our ancestral cathedral,
each stone added
onto living mortar,
placed atop two
stones beneath.

Your toil,
love's ash and slag,
with tears mixed,
forbid my fall,
grabbed my feet,
prevented my slip
into blunder's
abyss.

One day
I, too,
will lie beneath
the apex
to rest
in the shade
of family history.

CONVERSATIONS OF THE SOUL

To the future,
to our children,
to the stones coming -
may my love
endure like yours,
strength
solidified.
May I
their mortar
be.

Freedom

Ever since
I can remember, you
wave red, white and blue atop
our nation's splendor,
while helmeted boys
stand guard.

Each day
I rush past you,
fill my bag
with the goodies your defenders'
calluses can
buy.

I prosper
while young fighters
schlep fifty-pound packs
on furrowed backs.

War sand
'neath the straps of
their packs grind their shoulders
bloody; shoulders
built for lighter loads.

Seasoned
fighters in adolescent skin,
armed and allied,
they fight your bully,
often, to the
death;

CONVERSATIONS OF THE SOUL

    their would-be
   eighty years traded,
      so *you*,
    Freedom, can
    live another
       day.

    Those who've
 seen the muzzle flash
   understand the
cost to make you stand.
 They salute you with
    rifle in one
      hand.

     Tucked in
  blanket green, many
sleep; their mothers weep;
    beneath white
  rows of crosses, your
    keepers lie.

     Into the
  heartbeat of sunny
    Nine-Eleven,
  evil, in passenger
    jet-bombs,
      flew.

    Your arms
exploded in Manhattan; your
   insides blew out in
    Pennsylvania;
    your scalp
  in Washington DC.

ELIZABETH HELEN ROSE

The blasts
whirled us around to
watch, in horror,
you ablaze, hurling to
the ground!

Then,
through the smoke,
we saw young helmets, and
your colors, out of
human ashes,
rise.

We mourned
three thousand dead
while your
warriors stood
guard.

You, Freedom,
are the greatest gift, bought
with the greatest price.
Ground Zero drinks our
loved one's blood.

Today, we pause
to suspend the rush, to kiss
your defender's
ribboned breast; beneath which
lies their battle-scarred
chest.

September 11, 2001

Savior

Just in time
you've come.
Another moment and
I'd have died
in between
two rows of jagged teeth,
devoured by
the jaws of sin.

In waters,
deep within,
transgressors cruise;
pride, envy, anger,
to name a few;
silent predators of
my soul.

Elusive sharks,
their dorsal fins stay
submerged
till the strike.
Chomp!

My words bite.
Save me!
Without you,
my daily expeditions fail;
these marauders
maim.
They eat folks
up, alive.

CONVERSATIONS OF THE SOUL

Seize my shoulders,
yank me from the deep,
where fins circle.
Place my feet upon
The Rock
where
I can stand.

From transgression,
from offenses
past and present
transport me to your Eternal Crest
where, at last,
Your Arms of grace would
swallow me instead.

Fear

Always pickin'
on the little guy.
You intimidate the weak.
Ya' spineless bully;
meet someone your own size,
and ya' run.

Control freak!
When I don't cave in
to your thumb jabbed in me,
you reach into your
pocket of pranks.

You know how it works.
You ridicule.
My mental gears lock on.
We rotate.
Criticize me, long
enough, and your
hogwash I believe.

You badger me,
twist my arm behind my
back till I pay you homage; then
when, at last, I drop
on bended knee,
you flit away and laugh.

CONVERSATIONS OF THE SOUL

What do I do?
How do I escape from a
tyrant like you?
Who has the steel I need
to confront you?
Ha!

I found
The Armor.
One round from
his floor-to-ceiling arsenal
will smoke your
motor mouth
for good.
Meet My Savior.

Wisdom

No bidding.
Don't haggle here.
One-of-a-kind gems, like you,
can be bought,
but not with currency.

From a catalog,
from slick book pages, I can't
requisition you.
No glass case here.
Neither local merchant nor
tourist trap can
offer you.

In life's flea market,
amidst dusty hand-me-downs
and knockoffs,
scattered
and peddled cheap,
I can't snatch
you up for pennies.

You aren't
stockpiled, bought in
bulk, warehoused in a
supercenter.
No *Buy one-Get one free*
special.

CONVERSATIONS OF THE SOUL

In obscurity,
in life's back alley,
where suns don't rise
and rains don't fall;
where heaved cobblestones,
sprain, even young,
ankles, where
inclines seize breaths;

that's where I
stumble upon you,
crystal-encased boron,
a diamond worth ten times
more than
the average white.
You are
The Blue.

I pay for you
with hardship.
Full price.
And I, your loyal patron,
return.
Again and again.
Innocence and Ignorance
bring me.

~

Archer

Youngster,
lay down your arrow;
rest your bow.
Does one shoot first, then
search for the mark?

Clear the brush,
purge the elements
that block your vision,
impede your view.

Next,
pick your goal;
fix your sight;
consolidate all thought
into one objective.

By no
means, look back.
Never turn and get tangled
in the trivia behind
you.

Guard your today.
Watch for thieves who
kidnap your time, steal your
opportunities
for their
own non-ambition.

CONVERSATIONS OF THE SOUL

If your arrow
misses, should your attempt
go off course, don't fret;
load another toward
the bull's eye.

Now,
nock your arrow;
position your bow.
Pull back, hard; release.
Watch your effort,
toward
your future,
fly.

Sisters

There.
Like where evening
strolls to greet
morning,
like where midnight
kisses dawn,
so, go we,

two sisters,
different facets,
opposite horizons,
born of one
sky.

Nocturnal
metroscape, warm-white
twinkle lights on
chiseled black, you are a
New-York-midnight skyline,
of tranquility.

Daylight clamor,
variegated wildflowers that
litter cow pastures,
a Hokeytown sunrise
over unmanicured fields,
a rural frenzy,
that's me.

CONVERSATIONS OF THE SOUL

A contrast?
A disparity?
Perhaps.
Yet, Sister, who is
more alike
than you and me?

For Barb, 2000

Artist

Upon my
living frame,
over my beating heart,
my canvas
Your Fingers stretched.

Then up
to Your Easel,
upon your arms of grace
my naked form
You placed.

To a
due date,
just nine months, your
groundwork
You
confined.

You had
pigments to mill,
resins to blend,
special effects to
design.

You had
brushes to assemble,
techniques
to ponder,
a plan to
unfold.

CONVERSATIONS OF THE SOUL

Alas,
a few dabs
on your palette, and
You began
the portrait
of my soul.

Soulmate

Separate beings.
One heart.

Two brains.
One mind.

Diverse cultures.
One language.

Individual dreams.
One purpose.

Separate roles.
One performance.

Four hands.
One project.

Two colors.
One garment.

∼

1999

Obstacle

Had you
nothing better to do?
Did you possess no greater goal
than to block my way,
obstruct my
view?

On tiptoe
you made me stand.
Over your head, I had to stretch
my neck, strain to see
what lay
ahead.

I needed easy.
I wanted clarity,
but you? --you slapped me
with cluttered
perpetuity!

Off the
worn path, in isolation,
you made me roam.
I had to
encounter
undiscovered frontiers,
forge new trails.

ELIZABETH HELEN ROSE

I had to learn
to sprint up hill in order to
conquer the steep,
to grab roots and rocks
to keep from
falling.

Thank you.
I'm much obliged.
I found diamonds in
the dark.
I struck gold in
the gloom.

Did you
deprive or deliver me?
Did you stand in my way
or did you show me
the way?

At the
prospect
of journeying further,
without you,
I shudder.

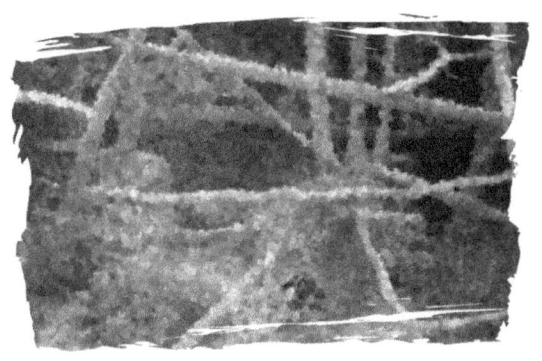

Papa

Beneath
white bushy brows your
ice-blue irises danced *the twinkle*,
and then they'd dance
with mine.

We laughed.
We cried.
We lingered on our
daddy-daughter dance floor
till death walked in,
clicked off the music and took
your hand from mine.

Papa,
with whom
will I waltz?
No one knows how.
Not like
you and I.

At your
hospital bed —death waits
with me; I press my wet cheek
to the dry riverbeds of your
laugh lines
There, my tear-river
flows.

CONVERSATIONS OF THE SOUL

Death
steps forward,
pockets your last exhale
and locks the swinging door
between us; your

laughter
sealed off,
your twinkle
interred.
But not forever.

***

Beneath young
blonde brows, in Heaven,
your ice-blue irises dance *the twinkle*,
and wait to dance
with mine.

For Leon Niemoczynski
1915-2003
Freedom Fighter
Gulag Labor Camp Survivor
His most often repeated phrase:
"It could be worse."

Graduate

Dear Sea Voyager,

You've arrived.
You may disembark.
Wave goodbye to your
adolescent self
who sails away
forever.

Up to now
Your family ship
has provided
for you -
staples, structure
and more.

Now,
you step ashore,
a land rover.
Get hiking boots.

Today
commissions
you as the only leader
of your future.

Meet
your new world.
Take title.
Uncharted ground
awaits your feet.

CONVERSATIONS OF THE SOUL

Take your blank scroll.
Untie its ribbon.
Map your course.
You have, in you, a lifetime
supply of ink.

Your timeline
awaits.
Your future
possesses no favorites.

It contains only
the you
beaten by or
triumphant over self.

Hardship
will barge in.
It will pull up a chair, sit
down and plop its
muddy boots
on your clean table.
Make friends.
The trespasser brings
treasure.

Into
negative winds
lean forward,
with your collar up and
feet spread.
Grab your
Creator's hand.

ELIZABETH HELEN ROSE

Befriend wisdom
and good colleagues.
Monitor and adjust your path so
the weak can follow you,
surefooted.

For Veronica,
High School Graduation, 2004

Husband

Beloved,
let the winds rage,
let the cyclone spin
the world
in fury.

Inside the
eye of our love, in the
quiet center
of the storm,
we thrive.

Let the
clouds bury the sun;
let them spit their hailstones.
Within love's shelter,
our sanctuary in the squall,
we recline.

CONVERSATIONS OF THE SOUL

Let thunder
crash; let lightning flash.
Within your arms of
sinew and sweat,
in nuptial sunlight,
I repose.

Beloved,
your vow,
love's golden strand,
secures me to
our rainbow as I hover over
water's surge
with you.

Should
the wind die,
should the storm lose
its eye, I shall
grieve for my center
of the tempest —
for you.

2004

Regret

I've not
a soul to blame,
no one to charge but me.
You pressed.
You nagged.
You posted warnings
all along youth's
highway.

So why
am I stuck?
How did I get caught?
In a mud flat.
In a quagmire.
In a quandary.

Sure I
rode the fast lane,
kept up with traffic,
horsed around,
had a good time,
hung out with the gang.

So
where's the gang now?
How come they've disappeared?
From my view.
Fled the scene.
Found a new
attraction.

CONVERSATIONS OF THE SOUL

Did I need
bigger signs?
Stronger prompts?
More of you to press
me?

Here I am
in the slow lane
with other gray hairs,
who discard
the quixotic notion,
the ideology,
that life's miles
can be accrued
without a few of you.

∽

Procrastination

Did I paint
today's canvas today?
Or did I not even pick up
His Paintbrush
in my hand?

Did I write
today's poetry today?
Or did I not pick up
His Pencil
in my hand?

Has today's yawn
sedated tomorrow's masterpiece?
Has the Master's Piece
even moved
my mind
today?

What details
will I leave forgotten?
What forgotten dream will
finally die?

Why write
His Request on my to-do list
at the bottom?
Why list trivia
at the top?

CONVERSATIONS OF THE SOUL

How long will
the Master's Hand
wait, empty?
How can
my empty hands
display my work,
undone?

Who will
sweat over my concoction
when my life ends?
How can another
concoct my work without
me?

When will I
have my fill of life's couch?
When has life's couch
ever filled me?

Will today's
rain check be valid tomorrow?
Will tomorrow turn
into another
rain-check day?

Don't I
want to hear Him say,
Well done, thou faithful servant?
Don't servants
serve?

ELIZABETH HELEN ROSE

Did I build
something good today?
Or did I not
even put His Hammer
in my hand?

Did I reach
one point on His map
today?
Or did I not
even put His atlas
in my hand?

Familiarity

For your hand,
for your warmth, my soul
reached up,
yesterday, but recoiled
at the unexpected
touch of a stranger's
chilly hand
instead.

Who's the alien?
I muttered.
*When did it
butt in?*
*Why did it sneak into
your space?*

I dread the
unpleasant-unfamiliar!
The stiff, the new, the tight,
the loose
of *who*, of *what* that
takes your place.

I want
exactly right.
Like today's
first-time-visitor
toddler-girl
whose Mama drags
her to the church nursery
and sneaks out
as her girl ogles toys,

ELIZABETH HELEN ROSE

I, too, must,
sometimes, be tricked
by life in order to
acclimate in the
unpleasant-unfamiliar.

The child in me
expects immunity from
things atypical.
The juvenile me craves
exemption from
the uncomfortable unknown.

I see timid me
in the toddler-girl who
reaches up for her Mama's hand,
with her eyes on the toys,
but grabs mine
instead;

then, looks up,
sees *my* face, recoils,
yanks, shrieks and runs for the
doorknob in a
continuum of ear-piercing
shrills.

I deplored yesterday,
when discomfort showed up.
The unexpected
could've asked,
solicited my permission.
Quite possibly - who knows – someday –
I may have - in due course
entertained their
proposal.

CONVERSATIONS OF THE SOUL

The peculiar
disjoints me,
severs me from kin.
It's my fear
that throws the tantrum,
the pain of the loss
of you.

That's why
I howl through the
uncomfortable,
run from the unsolicited.
It's my terror that yanks me
from discomfort, and
thrusts me to
the exit.

But egress doesn't
exist on Planet Earth.
Life propels us one way: Forward.
Toward chilly-fingered
strangers who grab
our hands
along the way.

If I snub
the unforeseen; if I reject
all the frigid hands;
if I refuse to warm their chill;
if I estrange rather than
espouse them,

then I,
forever diapered,
in an adult world, the
alien, remain.

Daughter

Into
human soil,
my youth's dirt,
my Spring meadow
freshly plowed,
God's finger poked you,
his tiny seed,
into,
not another heart,
but into mine.

Through
packed clay, some
of my Summer days a drought,
my mid-life heat bore
down, but
God's water reached
you.

Your
tender shoot
elbowed
grit and gravity, and,
inspite of them,
you grew! —
-inside,
not another heart,
but inside mine.

CONVERSATIONS OF THE SOUL

In
today's nip,
in my season's change,
my Summer green,
turned Autumn gold,
I, the garden,
thank The Gardener

for planting you,
his Sunflower,
my yellow-petaled chill chaser,
in,
not another garden,
but in mine.

For Jessica & Heather, 2005

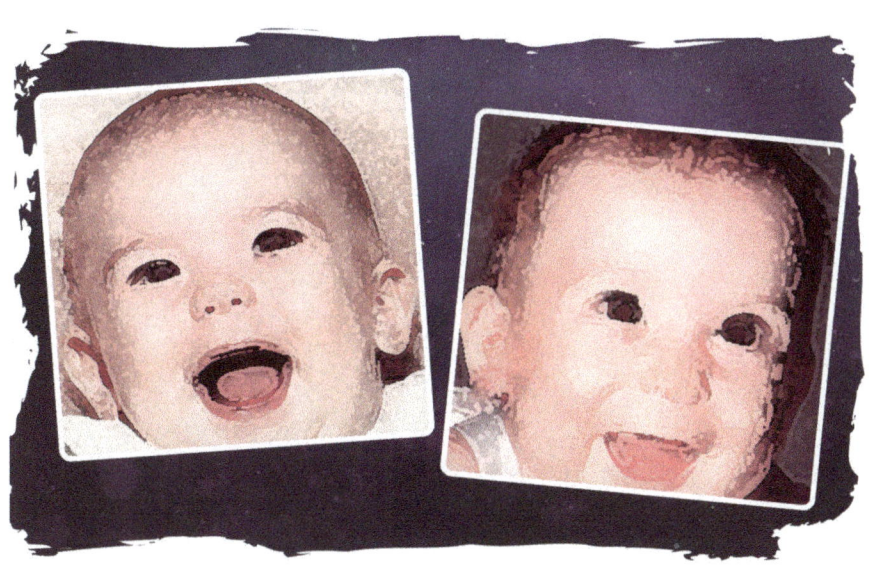

Joy

Hey kiddo,
how *do* you do it?
--dash in with a smile to
hug an old buzzard
like me?

What do *you* do
with the gook on *your* plate –
--the sorrow that
life dishes out, the grief that
gags grown men?

Too bad when you sit
your feet don't reach the floor.
You could run for office,
order all citizens to wear sneakers
with blinking lights.

You could issue
colored backpacks
with cartoon figures,
inoculate the public with
frown busters.

You could
mandate monkey bars,
see saws and
sliding boards at
clogged intersections.

CONVERSATIONS OF THE SOUL

Hey kiddo,
don't let life kick
your teeth out.
Keep your dash.
Keep your smile.
Don't grow
into an old buzzard
like me.

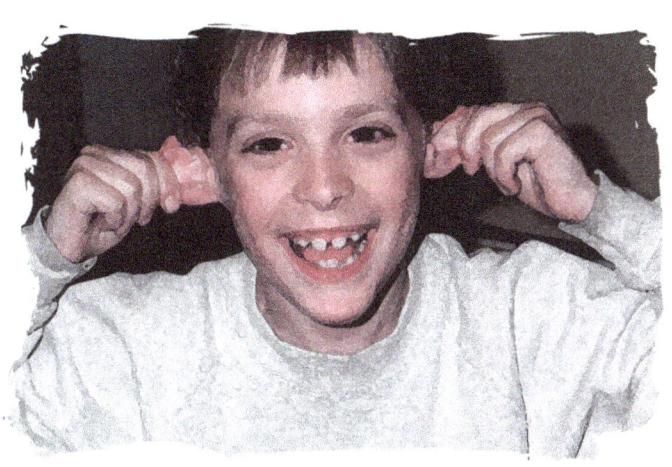

Courage

Submerged in frigid
impossibilities, that's you!
Like a crocus under snow!
Who else sprinkles
a colored
welcome mat
with longed-for petals, on a
blistery earth?

Ever hear
the phrase
small but mighty?
That's you!
You push ungloved fingers through
frozen ground, just to feel
the sun.

Dwarfed by those
who tower over you, *you*
take the lead; you
dare sleeping giants to wake up!

What muscled
oak offers its finger of a bud
to the frost to
welcome Spring?

What does
fear accomplish?
What monument
does cowardice inspire?
It huddles under cover till the
climate warms.

CONVERSATIONS OF THE SOUL

Not you;
you rise from your
bed and face life's north wind,
though naked and shaky.
You risk life and limb to
pronounce hope
to the others:
New life to come.

O Little One.
Stature doesn't delineate
one's height, one's depth, one's breadth.
God measures
by one's readiness to reach
from frozen ground,
to sprinkle longed-for petals
on a blistered earth.

∼

Accolade

If I pursue you,
if I eek, from me, one good deed,
just to taste your sweet,
I may as well drop
the word *good*
and call it what it is.
A deed.

Good means
superior, charitable, saintly.
Good sticks its hand out
to the crabs of
the world:
the work crab,
the family crab,
the church crab.

Good expects
to be pinched, but sticks its
hand out anyhow,
and doesn't
pinch back.

Good means
higher, taller, grander.
Good elevates the
loser who puts folks down,
bumps the winner up
another rung.

CONVERSATIONS OF THE SOUL

Good expects
to be knocked down, but lifts
the knockers
up anyhow, and never
knocks down.

Good means
greater, stellar, exceptional.
Good increases,
adds, multiplies – turns
grins to giggles,
giggles to guffaws,
guffaws to doubled-over,
belly-laugh
applause for the cause.

Good expects
to be diminished, but
multiplies delight in its subtractors
anyhow, and doesn't
diminish back.

Let me not
pursue *just* the sweet
of you,
though the human tongue
craves sweet.

Let me chase the
the bland, the insipid
taste of noble
that few tongues
prefer.

Death

Your finger
shuts my beloved's
mortal eye; you coffin his
earthly heart;
you bury his dust in
six feet of night;
but, inter love?
You cannot.

Your hand
cannot snatch love's
spirit hand.
Your greed
cannot seize love's
spirit wealth – our two hearts
entwined as one.
Love's heart
beats on,

beyond grave,
beyond words, beyond theft.
You may reach for, but
cannot snatch
love's spirit heart.

You may
shut, but cannot seal
love's spirit eye.
Love
lives on!

CONVERSATIONS OF THE SOUL

Love sees.
Love hears.
Love's hand penetrates
the veil
that separates
Heaven from Earth.

Love touches
its beloved from beyond.
One day, with spirit eyes, I'll
gaze, again,
at my beloved
who lives!

And together,
my beloved and I,
we'll watch The Creator
seal your eyes
and lower your coffin
to your grave
of eternal
night.

Forgiveness

You never falter,
never sway,
always big and steady
as a boulder -
-kind to the
unkind,

concerned with the
unconcerned;
you rally troops
for someone
who has never rallied
one finger for you.

Me?
One careless
shell from a shooting
mouth
wounds me
to chronic pain for
months.

You?
You cut
the bullet out,
cauterize the wound,
keep walking
and forget
who shot you.

Skin

Is it
too much to ask
for another
layer of you?

Maybe a
raincoat of joy for
when the black-cloud
folks blow in.

How about
a little leather? – a jacket
for my heart
so tongue thorns
can't pierce.

Or quilt batting,
epidermis quiltus,
to warm my soul when
the cold
shoulders me.

What about
a pink Tyvek®[1] wrap
for the gossip wind
against my
back?

I could
use a little tree bark,
too, for my tear ducts so
their sap
won't leak.

Or
bulletproof-glass
for when a
pointing finger
guns me.

Let's
do a layer of
reinforced concrete
when I get pulled
in opposite directions.

Or
bunker walls
for when
the bombs hit.

Ok. Ok.
Not the bunker
or the concrete…I just feel
better
for having shed
my old skin,

like a
snake who sloughs
off his injured
epidermis
covered in
burns or mites.

ahh…
I'm coming up,
soft now,
from
underneath.

Marriage

Mercy
Absolution
Responsibility
Reverence
Indemnity
Acquiescence
Generosity
Energy

Distributors

We humans
are distributors
of whatever we choose
to circulate.

Love, hate,
kindness, brutality…
We pass on
goods, ideas, lessons,
experiments…
from one entity
to another.

The
question is:
Who do we choose
as our
supplier?

Take
human gesture:
The shrug instead of the hug.
The smile instead of
the frown.

We
can distribute
no more or no less
than what
our chosen supplier
dispenses.

CONVERSATIONS OF THE SOUL

Who is
my supplier?
I can give, but only
mediocre stuff
from human pockets,
shallow.

When God supplies?
He supplies only
gilt-edged, state-of-the-art,
from sacred pockets,
deep.

Faith

The piety
your voice demands
from me,
right now, feels
bloody hard.

I limp, sweat-and-dirt
covered,
to the top of this
mountain you called me
to climb.

The peaks
and valleys, the blisters,
the backtracking -
my loaded
rucksack feels like a
boulder on
my back.

"Step off
the ledge; I'll catch you,"
you sibilate
from your far-away
Heaven,

once a near-by
restful blue,
now gray and black smoke,
like carbon monoxide
but I know it isn't.
Even
though I choke.

CONVERSATIONS OF THE SOUL

Your net,
below me, my mortal
eyes can't see.
I can
spout you,
shout you, throw you
to others
like parade candy;
but not to me.

Guess what?
I'm starring in my
very own
cliff hanger —
-the surgeon, the cliff
and me.

The ground
beneath my soles has
shifted beyond
supportable
and rattled the
spinal column of
my soul.

My fingers
lunge for the crack
in the cliff,
but finds it slick;
so, please
throw a rope down
from Heaven's Chopper
for me.

Contentment

Like a newborn
who smacks her lips after suckling
a belly-full of warm milk.
That's you.
Infant wonder exudes
from your
full-blown cataracts.

Your gnarled
fingers caress your precious
flickering moments,
like a babe fingers her mobile
which dangles over her
temporal crib.

Know
what I love about you?
Your purity.
Each day your attitude
shows up
baby-powder
fresh.

No hard crust,
baked over preconceived
judgement, no hands
up like a stop sign,
to keep folks at arm's length, no
been-there-done-that
growl.

CONVERSATIONS OF THE SOUL

No grizzle, just
your lovely oohs and aahs.
The hum-drum scenery
that my middle-age high-speed
commute ignores,
lights you up like
Christmas.

My bite of an
attitude needs your
newborn.
I need to powder
each morning baby fresh
like you.

I need to
suckle, with benediction,
each heart-warm
of a sunrise.

I need to
smack my lips over
each thirst-quench
of a sunset.

I need to
swig each blessing with
gratitude,
to seek the new in
what's old and
worn.

ELIZABETH HELEN ROSE

I need to
greet life, like you do, like a baby,
with my big eyes on
the bottle and
all of the wonder
within it.

For Selma F. Brand, 1911-2004

Fulfillment

Come,
Autumn breeze,
stroke the golden stalks of wheat
where my soul,
as a bucket, empty,
on its side,
lies.

Reach down;
here, to me, on the ground.
Rock my soul, the
hollow pail,
from side to side.

In my prime,
way back in my Spring,
the shiny brim of my bucket bustled;
its swollen brow emptied its
kernels to the
earth.

Now, rusty,
my brow sits silent,
its granary bare.
He who fills us up and
stands us all erect – each a different
shape and size – moves on.
To posterity.

ELIZABETH HELEN ROSE

Pity me? No!
Pity the unfortunate
vessel, the container that erodes,
upright, blessed
with seed, bulging with grain,
that never planted
a thing; but
sits buried in the
weeds.

Peace

When
trouble's hurricane
blew in; when its thunder
barraged my pleas; when the
wind shear of grief
tried to slice
my soul in half;

that's when
you and I met.
My sky rained razor blades,
sideways.
Sorrow bent me, like
a palm, in gale
force wind.

Finally,
the tempest passed.
Brute force
blasted out to sea.
That's when I
spotted storm veterans toppled,
trees much stronger
than me.

I stand because
Your Arms held me;
your whispers, in my ear, calmed me;
your shield defended
me.

CONVERSATIONS OF THE SOUL

Oh
Bosom of Bosoms!
Maker and Protector of my frail soul.
Pain almost snapped
the trunk of this tree, but you
steel fisted this storm
in the gut
and blew it far
from me.

Pillow **E**ncircle **A**bide **C**omfort **E**ase

Preserves

Like
twisting open
a Ball® canning jar
in January,
I open
my prayer journal
in my
soul's winter to savor
summer;

strawberries jammed,
grapes jellied,
tomatoes canned,
cucumbers pickled;
words written down,
preserved while fresh,
in ink on paper,
your answers
to my prayers.

Like canning,
preserving your miracles
makes me sweat.
My mental pot
boils over
in summer heat,
and in between
the canning?

CONVERSATIONS OF THE SOUL

I weed and harvest,
weed and harvest.
I bring in your blessings
by the
bushel baskets,
fuel for my faith to eat
when life's temperature
drops,

when gardens die,
when empty stalks
freeze over,
when the winds
of doubt howl
across my fields
buried
in white glaze,

when trees and faith
stand naked,
shaking in the cold.
These preserves,
sweet morsels written,
preserve me;
your Answers to my
prayers.

I read my
journal and taste
summer,
Your Strawberries,
Your Grapes, Your Tomatoes,
Your Cucumbers.

ELIZABETH HELEN ROSE

Then, as
one closes
the last empty jar the
following spring,
I close my journal,
and in the trees and in my faith,
buds sprout.
I see a new summer
with fresh
answers to new
prayers.

Winner,
Non-published Category
GPCWC, 2008

Notes

Acknowledgments

1. James M. Hunter, Evelyn Mackin, Anne D. Callahan, A. Lee Osterman, Terri M. Skirven; Rehabilitation of the Hand and Upper Extremity; 2002; St. Louis, Missouri; Mosby; Volume 1.

4. Anguish

1. https://en.m.wikipedia.org/wiki/Lignum_vitae. Slow-growing trees that produce highly valued wood, the densest and hardest wood known.

54. Skin

1. https://en.wikipedia.org/wiki/Tyvek - "…flashspun high-density polyethylene fibers, a synthetic material; trademark of the DuPont company, …often used as housewrap,

Index - Alphabetical

Accolade.......................... 146
Almost..............................76
Anger...............................12
Anguish..............................6
Archer.............................100
Artist 40
Baggage............................82
Childhood..........................18
Confusion...........................5
Contentment......................158
Courage...........................142
Daughter 134
Death.............................148
Distributors......................154
Dreams.............................22
Familiarity.......................131
Faith.............................156
Fear...............................96
Forgiveness.......................150
Freedom............................90
Friend.............................57
Fulfillment.......................161
Gift...............................68
Grace 14
Graduate 118
Hope 64
Husband...........................122
Journey............................29
Joy...............................138
Kindness 40
Love...............................52
Mama...............................34
Marriage..........................153

Index - Alphabetical

Music..............................62
Nature............................50
Obedience........................10
Obstacle.........................111
Pain................................1
Papa.............................114
Parents...........................86
Peace............................164
Prayer............................38
Preserves.......................166
Procrastination.................128
Regret...........................126
Savior............................94
Silence...........................63
Sin................................80
Sisters..........................104
Skin.............................151
Slander..........................27
Soul..............................32
Soulmate.......................110
Strength.........................48
Suffering........................60
Surrender.........................4
Time.............................56
Waiting..........................23
Wisdom..........................98
Words............................25
Youth............................44

Epilogue

In the summer of 2017, eighteen years after my Brachial Plexus surgery, I had the privilege of flying to Vietnam with Al and six other 'Nam vets who served in the I Corp area. Along with us came a few male college students and their history professor from Middle Tennessee State University and one other family member, a daughter of one of the vets. I'm grateful I was able to, physically, make this trip and visit the place from where Al and other young men were Medevac'd so many years ago.

Vietnam Battlefield Tours arranged the itinerary so that each veteran got to visit the area where they were stationed. I got to witness these 70-year-old vets step off the tour bus, look up, squint, look around for *their recognizable*. Though their hooches and mess halls had vanished, they'd dart to a spot in a field, in a jungle, in the sand of the South China Sea and point here and there. They'd discuss their positions, their duties, their fears — "their Vietnam," and I listened in awe with more respect for them today than ever.

On Memorial Day we stood beside the Perfume River and paid our respects to the American boys who died there—where no monument stands to remember them. As the vets stood in a semi-circle with tears running down their cheeks and read the names of their fallen buddies, I saw these vets as living, breathing monuments with the names of their buddies etched, not on stone, but on their hearts.

Pain changes a sufferer. It can soften us or harden us. It can open us up or shut us down. We thank God for His healing hands on both of us. We are grateful for His mercy and his continual restoration in each of us every day.

Here are a few photos from this memorable trip.

CONVERSATIONS OF THE SOUL

ELIZABETH HELEN ROSE

About the Author

Her full name fills, even a large, mouth - Elizabeth Helen Rose Niemoczynski Schaarschmidt. Hence the pruned name for publishing.

Elizabeth is a bi-lingual, born of Polish refugee Nazi and Gulag labor camp survivors in 1948. Her early childhood took place on St. Anne's Avenue in the Polish section of South Bronx, where she attended St. Adalbert's Catholic School till 5th grade. When the family of eight moved to Brass Castle Road in Oxford, New Jersey, she went to White Township Elementary and Phillipsburg Catholic High School. After commencement, in 1966, she returned to New York, graduated from Mary Byers Executive Secretarial program and worked for John Blair & Company in Manhattan.

In 1967 she met the love of her life on a blind date, then Corporal Allen Schaarschmidt, just back from Vietnam, a USMC double-purple heart almost-amputee who limped, walked with a cane and smoked Lucky Strikes. They married, had two beautiful daughters and a personal experience with God.

After Allen graduated from United Wesleyan College, in theology, they founded Blessed Hope Church of the Nazarene in Phillipsburg, New Jersey where Allen became the pastor. The year was 1980.

Elizabeth went on to study voice and piano at United Wesleyan and became the church's Music Director. Years later, when she could no longer play the piano, she accepted her husband's invitation to be Ministry Director.

Elizabeth is a devoted Pastor's wife, loving mother, grandmother and great-grandmother. She is a dedicated and much-loved ministry, youth and worship leader. Her Sunday morning reflections, spiritual lessons taken from everyday life, stir up both laughter and tears. The gifted storyteller has now developed into an accomplished, YouTube-taught, artist.

Her life scripture is Psalm 84:5-7 "Blessed are those whose strength is in you, whose hearts are set on pilgrimage. As they pass through the Valley of Baka [tears], they make it a place of springs…They go from strength to strength, till each appears before God in Zion."

To her pain, her daily companion, she says *Thank You*. She often drinks cold coffee because she's too busy prattling about, dictating thoughts into her laptop, working on her purpose, shoving pain out of the way.

Elizabeth Helen Rose is an emerging poet and author of meditations, prayers and memoirs. *Conversations of the Soul* is Elizabeth's first book, a debut collection of her poetry. *The Pain Monster's Gift* is her second book, a memoir of her journey through Brachial Plexopathy's Valley of Sorrow.

Website & Booking: www.elizabethhelenrose.com

Author photo by Jessica Faenza

facebook.com/elizabethhelenrose

twitter.com/elizabethhelenrose

instagram.com/elizabethhelenrose